Voyager

Poems From A Journey

John S. Langley

Copyright © 2023 J. S. Langley

The right of J. S. Langley to be identified as the Author of the Work has been asserted by him in accordance to the Copyrights, Designs and Patents Act 1988.
The Copyright for each poem resides with the author. All images are the property of the author or freely available in the public domain.

First Published in 2023 by LV Publishing

Apart from any use permitted under UK copyright law, this publication may only be reproduced, stored in a retrieval system, or transmitted, in any form, or by any means, with prior permission in writing of the publisher or, in the case of reprographic production, in accordance with the terms of licenses issued by the Copyright Licensing Agency.

All characters and events in this publication, other than those clearly in the public domain, are fictitious and any resemblance to real persons, living or dead, is purely coincidental.

Print ISBN: 978-1-7391381-5-8

Voyager is mainly about a cruise we took from Santiago to Buenos Aires via Tierra del Fuego and Cape Horn. We didn't know what to expect, our minds a jumble of images of the luxury of modern cruise ships and school-day memories of tales of exploration, discovery and shipwrecks associated with this marine seaway, treacherous and unpredictable, that includes the most southerly continental point before Antarctica.

At our time of life we figured that if we were ever going to do it, it had to be soon. After all what could possibly go wrong...?

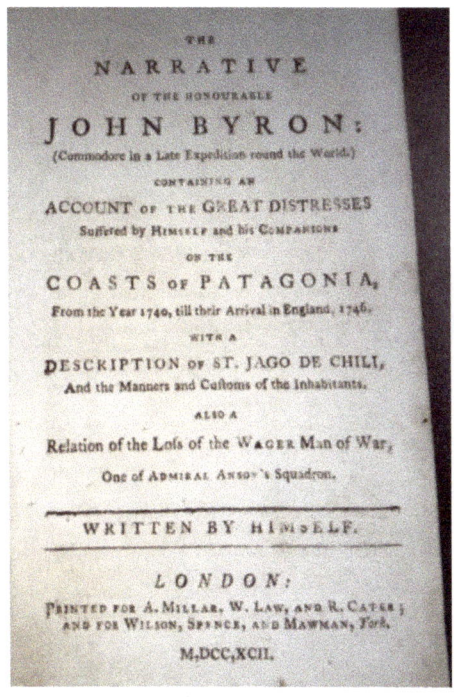

John S. Langley

To our sons – Robert, Iain, & Michael
their partners Sophie, Laura, & Kirst, and
our grandchildren Abbie, Ben & James
who brighten up our lives, and to my
long-suffering wife, Janet,
my travelling companion
through life..

Always remember: "The journey is as important as the destination."

CONTENTS

I. BEFORE THE OFF   Page

   1. Harsh but True   2
   2. Morning!   4
   3. Starting off   5

II. SANTIAGO (Chile)

   4. Arrival and Survival   8
   5. Exploration   10
   6. New Year's Eve   12
   7. New Year in Santiago   14
   8. One Road   16
   9. Feeding Frenzy   18

III. ONBOARD

   10. Balcony   22
   11. We are   24
   12. Narrow   26
   13. Sea-watching   27
   14. People You Meet   28
   15. Navigation by Loos   30

IV. PUERTO MONTT

16.	Scenery and Souvenirs	32
17.	Travelling South	40
18.	Still Natural?	41

V. PUERTO CHACABUCO

19.	10.000 Steps	46

VI. AT SEA

20.	The Naming of Things	52
21.	Hace Bastante	54
22.	Still Roving	56
23.	Broken Coast	57
24.	Identifying	58
25.	White Water	60
26.	Albatross Airborne	62
27.	Trust in Strangers	63
28.	Different and the Same	64

VII. PUNTAS ARENAS

29.	Mosaic	68
30.	Glacier Alley	75

VIII. USHUAIA (Argentina)

31.	Kicking up a Dust Storm	82
32.	Getting up Close	88

IX. AROUND THE HORN (Chile)

33.	Cape Horn	95
34.	Rolling Along	98
35.	SKI-ing	99

X. THE FALKLAND ISLANDS (UK)

36.	Approach	102
37.	War	105
38.	Kathryn	113
39.	Gifts	114
40.	Farewell	116
41.	Later	117

XI. AT SEA AGAIN

42.	Course Correction	120
43.	Right Decision?	122
44.	Change of Direction	124

XII. PUERTO MADRYN (The missed stop)

45.	At Last	127
46.	The Stop We Missed	128
47.	Walking	130
48.	Position on the Map	132
49.	Something They Agree On	134
50.	The Lift Expert	136

51.	Dinner Conversation	139
52.	Parasitic Jaeger	140
53.	Sorry	142

XIII. MONTEVIDEO (Uruguay)

54.	Not What We Expected	144
55.	Sizes	146
56.	We Scratch the Surface	147
57.	The Last Ones	150
58.	Covid	152

XIV. BUENOS AIRES (Argentina)

59.	Disembarkation	156
60.	There's only one thing	159

XV. Going Home

61.	Knowing When To…	161
62.	Taking for Granted	162
63.	Back	164

XVI. REFLECTIONS

64.	Leisure Domes	168
65.	Is it not so?	169
66.	What have we learnt?	172

Magellanic Penguin

BEFORE THE OFF

John S. Langley

Harsh but True

I was home for the weekend
waiting to catch a bus into Newcastle
the Number 49 - that arrived at last
with another right behind it

An old lady was also waiting
a little unsteady on her feet

I recognised her
she was from the very next street
to me but it had been a while
since I'd seen her

I held out a hand
helped her onto the bus

She was more frail
than I remembered
but no less outspoken

We sat side by side
'Bus fares today!' she said
'It's scandalous. Do they
think we're made of money?'

We chatted on
'You're not from round here.'
she said. It was not a question
It was a statement

Voyager

They were only a few words
but they bit deep

She clearly didn't recognise me
Had I changed so much?

I was from the next street
but I'd travelled
I'd had to re-mould my accent
to avoid ridicule
prejudice
and to be understood

My roots were still here
but I had grown new branches
I was from round here
but also I wasn't - anymore

What she said was harsh
but it was also true.

John S. Langley

Morning!

I always sneeze in the morning
I think it's my body saying
'Get up you lazy git
a new day has dawned
full of new opportunities'

I try to ignore it.

When I sneeze
my whole body shudders
breath is expelled
at explosive speeds
and the volume of sound
that comes out
I would struggle to make
at any other time.

What is this all about?

I am shaken
into wakefulness

Am I alone in this phenomenon
or am I just allergic to mornings?

Starting off

The drive South was horrendous even though we stopped off in Manchester, in an hotel that was locked and wouldn't let us in because of a "security incident"

Over 10 hours it took us to get to Heathrow, the train strikes driving people onto the roads con-
-gestion and rain doing the rest. But we did see 2 grandchildren

for an hour or two before worrying about Border staff strikes, Covid rules on British Airways and flight cancellations. So when we finally were in our seats we were amazed.

Now there was only 14 hrs and 40 minutes to go before we were due to land in a different hemisphere time zone and season.

We ate, we drank, watched movies and tried to get some sleep.

John S. Langley

Voyager

SANTIAGO (CHILE)

30th Dec 2022 - 1st Jan 2023
32ºC Sunrise: 06:37hrs   Sunset: 20:26hrs

John S. Langley

Arrival and Survival

We have arrived! It is our first time in Chile. Our first impressions are that we were wrong, preconceived ideas of a relatively poor country are completely wide of the mark!

Santiago is modern, developed and developing putting our expectations to shame. I guess that's one reason you travel - to be corrected.

Everything is new to us, we begin to get used to the -3hr time difference to speaking the wrong language, to longer days, warmer temperatures to being on holiday.

At the hotel, better than Heathrow we try and fail to know how to order a meal, wrong-footed by the use of QR codes.

Voyager

There are no menus at the bar, you
have to connect to the hotel internet
then use your smartphone to read
the QR code and access the menu

and prices. Then you can make your
choice, place your order and voila! In
our room no instructions. Another
QR code is embedded in the table

But we're ready now, know what
to do. We have arrived. Are here.
And, with the help of the QR codes
we can survive.

Exploration

In the hotel they are preparing to party.
$300 a head for a New Year shindig
that we're not invited to.

We go on a city tour warned beforehand
no valuables, no jewellery, be aware, be
careful. Scared us to death

which I guess was the objective. The guide
says we will stop and get out as long as the
police are present

We stop. The police are happy to pose for
selfies with American tourists. We are in a
fog as we are told too much to hold on to

history, politics, culture, and we stop to see
parliamentary buildings, the cathedral, and
our guide says the best Chilean red is
Carménère.

Voyager

John S. Langley

New Year's Eve

We venture out alone after a breakfast buffet
and go shopping, battling to communicate
realising how out of our depth we are

But we need wine to celebrate New Year! So
we soldier on with help from locals who do
not scoff and manage to buy a bottle of fizz

and, most importantly, a Carménère. Then
we seek out some food. Fresh cheeses and
ham and bread. Only one thing is missing

Sacacorchos, a corkscrew. We didn't know
the word then but mimed the action, were
understood but still couldn't find one

After shopping we carried the bags to Cerro
San Cristobal, an 860 meter hill. We climbed
it in a cable car after buying a light lunch.

At the summit a tremendous view and a
statue of the Virgin Mary that overlooks the
city on all sides.

Back in the hotel we settle in to see in the
New Year. I dig out the cork from the wine
bottle with a nail file. It takes about an hour.

We watch on the TV as the New Year moves
around the world: Auckland, Sydney, Dubai,
London. We watch the fireworks, marvel at
the drones, flying in formation.

We text home. Nearest & dearest. Get replies!
Global connectivity in action. We wait for local
midnight in another 3 hours. There are no
fireworks they've banned them this year.

It's Jan 1st 2023, today we board!

Voyager

John S. Langley

New Year in Santiago

What am I doing here?
This is **not** a philosophical question
I mean what am I doing **here**
in Santiago, Chile, South America
in this other hemisphere
where everything is upside down

I'm normally in my back garden
with a group of lively others
alcohol infused and ready to sing
waiting for the chimes that mark
both an end and a beginning

the moment to light
the blue touch paper
and run to safety before
the boxed firework display
explodes into loud colours
fizzes, whizzes and bangs

But instead, this year end
we decided to go adventuring
3 years later than planned
We had decided that
it was going to have to be
now or ...

Voyager

John S. Langley

One Road

On the one fast road from Santiago
to San Antonio on the Pacific coast.

A few birds appear and disappear in
morning mist, full of welcome moisture.

We are slowed by 3 accidents along
the way, flashing blue and red lights.

A grey van passes us on the inside
the driver's hand reaching out to
hold his broken back bumper on
the roof, steering with the other

We pass areas of agricultural land
wetted by the Miapo river, growing
grapevines, onions, plums, walnuts...

Then the blockages clear away
and we drive on towards the coast
in bright sunshine
                      and high expectations.

Voyager

John S. Langley

Feeding Frenzy

As the ship leaves port
the waters are stirred
and black-backed gulls
of a lesser variety
come out of nowhere
flock, dive, feed
on whatever we have disturbed
attacking each other
for the choicest morsels

It is soon over.
The birds disperse
as we sail away

...

The next morning
we go for a buffet breakfast.
There are many choices
layered, stacked or stirred
and lots of people
of all varieties
who, like us, appear
to come out of nowhere
and flock, push, and dive
to feed on what is laid out
competing with each other
for the choicest morsels

It is soon over.
The buffet closes at 11:00 am
and we all disperse
and sail on.

Voyager

John S. Langley

Voyager

ONBOARD

John S. Langley

Balcony

Not all of us have a balcony
for those of us who do
I think it behoves us
to make the most of it

So I sat out in the glaring sun
the strong and gusting wind
the heaving of the swelling waves
to see what I could see

and all I could see was the sea.
Although there was land out there
that I could see on the cabin tv
and the live satellite tracking.

But if I chose to ignore all that
and just rely on my senses
the sights, the smells, the sounds
the feel and taste of the air then

it seemed as if we were all alone
adrift on a planet full of water
too wet and cold for us to survive
but as alluring as the Siren's song.

I went inside to switched on the tv
to be reassured by the digital map
because it's better to think that you
know where you are than to get
yourself all in a flap.

Voyager

John S. Langley

We are

We are the medicated
we live beyond our years
we take pills as directed
till they come out of our ears

Spending our children's money
we keep well out of their way
I'm sure they'll see it's a blessing
when we say we've had a good day

We see things over and over
History repeating and such
wondering if we'll ever learn
not being listened to much

So we go on a cruise, to take in the world
and marvel at where we can roam
transported and feted and fed every day.
It's less than the price of a care home!

Voyager

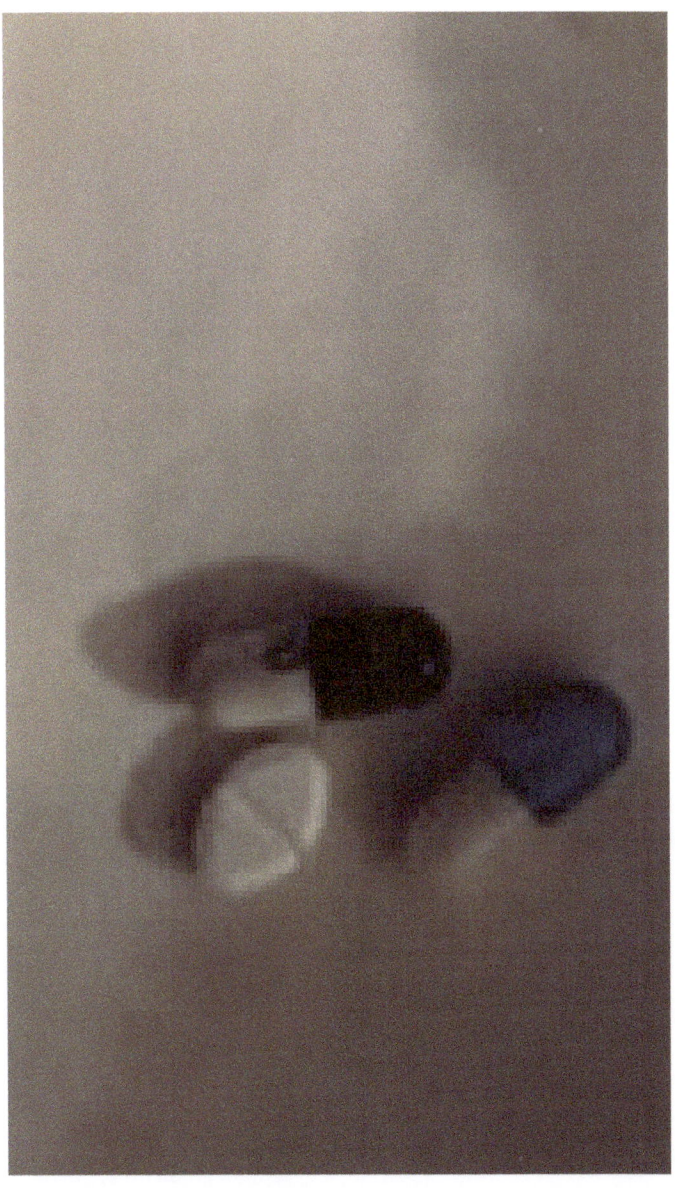

John S. Langley

Narrow

Chile is a narrow land
bordered by mountains and sea
hot in the North
cold in the South
foreign to you and to me

We come from the other side of the globe
where, just for a start
it's cold in the North
and hot in the South
but are we really such poles apart?

Sea-watching

Just to sit and watch the sea
from a balcony aboard a ship
however contrived the experience
is therapeutic to the soul

The rhythmic roll of the journey
the feathering white of the breakers
the tightrope walk of the Shearwaters
skimming over the shifting surface

The chance of the unexpected.
An albatross, a dolphin, or petrel.
The unnoticed passing of time
as your mind relaxes and senses refocus

It becomes a wakeful dream, salt air brushing
your face. Harsher weather may be coming
seen in the distance, grey on grey, there is
rain falling though there is time yet
                   before you have to go inside.

People You Meet

I remember when I was in Gib
said the man who spoke very glib
I walked all day long
for a laugh and a song
but now I can't run or I'll trip.

There was a young lad from Peru
who said, 'Hey, How do you do?'
I said I was fine
then I did a small mime
of someone who hadn't a clue.

Two people who'd cruised quite a lot
had Platinum points in their pot
they got the best treatment
while we got passed by
but we didn't care, not a jot
(Well not much anyway!)

Voyager

From Texas, Idaho, California
Colorado, Maine, Florida
they flock from the States
along with their mates
going South for the Winter, oh yea!

We Brits travel far, the Swedes do as well
coming from well... you never can tell
we smile at each other
you'd think we were brothers
even though we've got nothing to sell.

So on cruises it pays to be friendly
to talk to each other correctly
there'll be some that like you
and others who won't
but be sure to be nice to the crew.

John S. Langley

Navigation by Loos

Those of us with weak bladders
need special kinds of maps
that do not feature elevations
nor the normal points of interest
but where the nearest toilets are
and whether they are free or not
and, if at all possible, a warning
of their likely cleanliness

The first word we learn
in any new language is not
'Hello', 'Thank you' or 'Breakfast'
essential though these may be
but the word for TOILET
Baños, Toilette, Toalett, 洗手间

You will see us comparing notes
before running, waddling or queuing
at each opportunity that presents itself.

Maintaining a less than full bladder
is the secret of a happy life!

PUERTO MONTT

3rd Jan 2023
16ºC   Sunrise: 06:23hrs   Sunset: 21:28hrs

John S. Langley

Scenery and Souvenirs

A fishing port
the smell hits you first
of dead fish
or a sea lion's breath

We travel through
the town graffiti
peeling paint
on old wood
giving way
to clean streets
and new apartments
where virgin forest
used to be
a bare two hundred
years ago
impenetrable
but now gone
the wood burnt
or used to build
or be exported.

We drive along
a lakeside
a fresh water heaven
carved deep
by ancient ice flows

Voyager

First stop
is Petrohue Falls
where emerald green water
torrents through
and over
volcanic rock
spuming white
crashing down
in places placid
and crystal clear

John S. Langley

The tops of the volcanoes
are hidden in cloud
they are so tall they make
their own weather
Our tour guide tells us
there is less snow each year
the glaciers are melting.
They have no solution
but watch it happening.

Voyager

The bus growls diesel
as it snakes up
the steep slopes
of a serpent road
and we enter the cloud layer.
Osorno volcano
still snow-capped
rising to 8,700 feet.

Here we stop, having left
the sun behind us.
It is a white-out.
We are disoriented
people appear
and disappear
out of the mist
like ghosts.

Volcanic rock; black
porous, red, half-frozen
crunches underfoot.
On a different day the views
are, apparently, spectacular.
Today the better view
was further down
before we hit the cloud.
Here we glimpsed
the spectacular peak
but didn't stop
the need to obey

John S. Langley

the rules of the itinerary
being paramount.

Voyager

Going back down
thick forest borders
the road on either side
for a stretch.

A small reminder
of what there once was.
I am almost sure
that as our forebears
stripped away the trees
they did not know
that they were
ripping out
their own lungs
as well.

Now
we do know
and we still do it
which has got to be worse.

We descend
to a glorious lakeside lunch
begun with a Pisco Sour
and then four courses
accompanied by water
wine, and finally coffee.

John S. Langley

Talking to fellow travellers
we share pictures
of our grandchildren.

Back in Puerto Varas
on the shores of Lake Llanquihue
we visit hotel restrooms

and search for souvenirs
in sunshine and warmth.

I do not know how to feel
pleased at having seen
and contributed a little money?
Smiling when they talked
proudly of development
new apartments, tourism
and increasing wealth?
Or was I simply culpable
by association
somehow participating
in an ongoing natural decline
I should have been
raging against?

We return
to the comfort of the Ship
to eat more food
be entertained
and burn some more oil.

Voyager

John S. Langley

Travelling South

The days lengthen
the temperature drops
the sky descends
to meet the mountains
that rise out of the sea

And we see few lights
between our destinations
little evidence of people
and strangely the world
looks as though it does
not mourn the omission
nor hanker after
greater exploitation
...

Still Natural?

We could not have come to this area
any other way; at this time, at our age
but do we deserve the privilege?
Is our individual awe and satisfaction
enough justification for our trespass?

Sailing through the Fiordo Aisen
(past Isla Elena towards Chacabuco)
trees cling to cliffs and higher
in the sunlight, above the clouds
are the tops of mountains, glaciers.

We pass only fish farms
the area is magnificent
in its stark beauty.

I know I could not disembark
and survive here
Good!
Is this the closest I will get
to a world not yet overrun*
by human expansion
and the concrete
that we bring?

(*I learn later that even this area has
been touched, torn and transformed)*

John S. Langley

I stop thinking such dour thoughts
and immerse myself in my senses
Just look
Just listen
Just feel
Just hear
Just taste the air
Oh, wow!

It is a meditation
that in stillness
cleanses

When I am full
when I am overfilled
I retreat back into
my man-made
metal shell
conflicted.

I am both relaxed
and vexed.

Voyager

Voyager

PUERTO CHACABUCO

4th Jan 2023
23ºC   Sunrise: 06:09hrs   Sunset: 21:42hrs

John S. Langley

10,000 Steps

A 2 hour walk
in a Nature Reserve
that conserves rain forest
or re-constituted rain forest
after the land was apportioned
as if we had the right
to burn or cut down.

Even here 10,000's
of people live mainly based
around the fishing industry
salmon farms

But there is a kind of hope
land handed back for conservation
and perhaps our tourist dollars
confirm some kind of value.

We walk following a river
through thick vegetation
hearing birds but not seeing
except for a fluttering glimpse
the fluted call of the Diucon

Voyager

John S. Langley

After the walk there is Pisco Sour
barbecued lamb and dancing.
If this is what it takes to save
the planet
two steps back
one step forward
I'm all for it.

At least it's not
making things
considerably worse.

Voyager

John S. Langley

Voyager

John S. Langley

The Naming of Things

We pass a bay
of shipwrecks
the Golfo de Penas
and inland ice fields
that we cannot see

Mist rises and falls
shrouding visibility
and we drift closer then
further from the shore

For us it is the first time
here, probably the last
but it is easy to imagine
how Darwin, Fitzroy

were inspired and found
new species to European
science, but long known
to the local inhabitants

and gave names to things
discovered again, their
own names latinised, or
of places or people well-

recognised by them who
had the power of the pen
and now these names
have stuck
recorded for all
within a book.

Voyager

John S. Langley

Hace Bastante

We go to the
breakfast buffet
There is almost
nowhere left
to sit, except to
share a space
with a man
whose chiseled face
had features
I had time to muse
that could make you an offer
you couldn't refuse.

He spoke no English
We spoke no Spanish
But it was only polite
to chat
So we conversed on this
and also on that

He was from Chile
Santiago in fact
and when he asked
using fair tact
where we were from
we said England
He smiled and
drew a line in the sand
by asking, 'Londres?'
to which we said, 'No'

Voyager

and said 'Carlisle'
to which he said, 'Oh?'

He tried to teach us numbers
uno, tres and dos
our awful lack of Spanish
was clearly our loss
He taught us how to ask
how much 'Cuanto vale'
and eventually said
that's enough 'Hace bastante'
then he shook my hand
I said 'Buenas dia'
he smiled, shook his head
and left the cafeteria

I will never know if
his gesture meant goodbye
or if he'd lost all hope
even though we were willing to try.

Isla Byron
Based on Byron's Poem 'So, we'll go no more a roving'

Still Roving

So, we'll still go a roving
Till late into the night
With hearts that still are loving
Beneath a moon that's still as bright
For our footfalls fall in health
And our soul beats in our breast
Though our hearts need pause to breathe
All our love has still to crest
Days and nights are made for proving
That our time is gone too soon
Yet we'll still go on a roving
By the light of our fitful moon.

Broken Coast

We sail past a broken coast
waves towering white
amongst scattered rocks
dangerous for shipping

How do these stones
survive such a pounding
and keep their sharp edges
dangerous for mounting

And, as soon as salt will allow
there is green, low and covering
black rock, roots seeking fissures
dangerous for tripping

Too many islands, too many inlets
too many tops with cloud covering
impossible to imagine it's charted
dangerous for mapping

And we sail past, on a gentle swell
now aware of such a place existing
just as the first explorers did
dangerous for knowing

John S. Langley

Identifying

What is that bird?
As big as a small plane
or glider more like
skimming the waves
wingtip seeming to scratch
the sea surface as it passes

A white body, wings black atop
and mottled underneath
should surely be distinctive
but we have no identification
guide. We see only the bird.

Did the Mariner have a guidebook?
Do we need to hang the lack of
an officially recognised sighting
around our necks?

It is a beautiful thing
at one with its environment
giving us a moment's pleasure
in our seeing

Voyager

although I am sure
it does not watch
us watching

- if it did
I wonder what name
it would give us?

John S. Langley

White Water

White water follows our leaving
a churned up turbulent wake
in lanes of engine determined
consistency.

As it recedes into the distance
synonymous with the time of
first formation, it begins to break
hydrodynamic-ally

And far away, further than we can see
standing at the stern, the whiteness
dissolves back into opaque waters
the far reaching blue-grey mass

that returns to its natural frequency
of ebb and flow, driven by mightier
powers, and continues as if
we had never been there.

Voyager

John S. Langley

Albatross Airborne

Like a jumbo jet lumbering into flight
legs racing, pushing, one-two, one-two
against the water surface, wings extended
gathering wind under aerodynamically
evolution-engineered feathered surfaces
in an attempt to defy gravity.

The effort is extreme, the knowledge that
perseverance of this ungainly gait will bring
success innate, and once airborne, once
back to being a part of its natural element
the majesty of effortless flight is clear, the
clumsiness of takeoff forgotten.

Voyager

Trust in Strangers

The sea was a bit choppy last night
out of the channels, in the Pacific
but what can you do, you can't get off!

So you hold on, trusting the engineers
who designed this Ship, got the centre
of gravity right, that the craftsmen (and
women) who riveted it together were
skilled enough to prevent leaks

that the crew navigating, controlling
speed and direction are experienced
and motivated.

There's nothing else you can do but
put your trust in strangers, hold on
and hope for the best.

John S. Langley

Different and the Same

The landscape
has become Scandinavian
hard bare rock protruding
through low green.

We sail down coastal fjords
The world is turned upon
its head, geography repeated
the same but different.

Later the mountain tops
become sharp grey and free
of vegetation, places where
snow clusters, compacted

in white patches, glistening
in this Summer sun, this hard
but beautiful land, different
but the same.

Voyager

PUNTA ARENAS

7th Jan 2023
11ºC Sunrise: 05:29hrs   Sunset: 22:10hrs

John S. Langley

Mosaic

We enter a Ghost town
It is a Saturday
We have a photograph
of a street map
on our phone
The streets are clean
we feel safe
and we are lost.

The place we are going
is no longer there
That's the trouble
with Guides
they are too soon
out of date.

In the central square
we find people
wide roads
slow traffic
green men at crossings.

We find out that there
are three main things
that keep this area going:
Sheep
Oil
Tourism
in that order...

Voyager

We visit a reproduction
of Magellan's 'Victoria'
the 1 in 5 that made it
all the way home though
he was left
part way
behind.

And alongside
a reproduction
of 'The Beagle'
with Darwin's name
surpassing Captain Fitzroy's
in the hardboard chronicles.

How did men survive so long
in such small spaces
on treacherous
and unknown seas?
Perhaps because that
once begun they didn't
have a choice.

We look over water
now clearly labelled
the 'Straits of Magellan.'

On maps there are names
of people now remembered
through being labelled
on waters or land.

John S. Langley

Back in the Central Museum
we read that Chile plans
to reduce it's reliance
on fossils fuels by 8%
by 2040 compared to 2018.
With so much wind
and hydro possible
I can only shake my head
in disbelief.

The indigenous people
are recorded in relics
and dioramas
bartering food
and leather
for metals
and alcohol
and Christianity
Recognised
Usurped
'Educated'
Subservient
Proud
    … a complex picture?

History is portrayed
room by room
Magellan
The penal colony

Voyager

Shackleton
Scott
Darwin, Fitzroy
Oil and Gas
Fauna and Flora

And outside
in the central square
(again)
a statue with
Magellan atop
Indigenous people
underneath
European over local
And even now
the remaining ancestors
protest
Not through blood
Not through violence
But by throwing black paint
at the statue
Only some of which
is cleaned away.

We buy jumpers
and jewellery
with pieces of paper.
The stall holders
seem happy
with the exchange.

John S. Langley

One shakes my hand.
I check I still have my watch.

Back on the Ship
our ordered food
is dropped
and we are placated
with a copious supply
of Chilean Sauvignon Blanc

And after all that
in the theatre
the entertainment is
'The History of the Tango'
and practical demonstration
still sensual
after it's birth
100-ish years ago
in the brothels
of Buenos Aires.

Which all goes to prove
that life is like
a box of chocolates
without a guide.
You just don't know
what you're going
to get
next.

Voyager

John S. Langley

Glacier Alley

We are waiting for the
glaciers to appear when
a pod of Orcas blow!

Yes, Killer Whales!

A pod of 4-6
a lifetime ambition
secretly held
to see them in the wild
surprisingly fulfilled.

And there are other
mysteries that break
the surface for a second
splash
and are gone.

There are birds
too far away to identify.
Stone worn peaks
with fractured snow
and sunshine

and a light wind.

We are in the 'Beagle Channel'
Cordillera Darwin to the North
the small Isla Darwin to the South

John S. Langley

We follow our progress with a map
eco-friendly, made out of stone.

We spot a pair of South American
Terns; sharp-edged, streamlined
shrieking, as they pass close by.

There is ice in the water.

Glaciers named after countries
Spain
      Germany
            Italy
               Holland
a backdrop of high mountains
hold back the clouds like a
breaking wave of white horses.

The air is clear, crisp with cold
even in this warmest of seasons.

This land of glaciers
looks magnificent from a distance
the comfort of a heated room behind us.

But if we were in it, not onlookers
it would be a harsh place to live
hard to survive amongst such
rugged, shifting beauty.

Voyager

John S. Langley

As if to underline our thoughts
two Turkey Vultures emerge
from nowhere
spiral far overhead
sweep across the sky
and are gone.

Glacier Italia:
As we watch, pieces of ice
break away and fall into the sea
How long has it taken this ice to
form, to travel to the edge for us
to see the moment of the splash!?

Ice crystals on the water surface
cause it to sparkle as sunlight hits
and the glacier shines ice blue
in this Summer sun.

It is a truly breathtaking spectacle.
If people cannot travel into space
and look backwards to realise
the beauty
        and fragility
                of the world
    then come here
        and marvel
            and maybe
   realise, in the same way
what we have
       and that we should work
   to not throw it away!

Voyager

USHUAIA
(oosh-why-ya)
ARGENTINA
(Day 8)

8th Jan 2023
23ºC   Sunrise: 05:10hrs   Sunset: 22:09hrs

John S. Langley

Kicking up a Dust Storm

Red-faced we've caught the sun
The Unions are striking in Ushuaia
and we cannot land. Each to each
their rules and we are but flotsam
in this war.

We see grey Argentinian Navy and
Antarctic expeditionary vessels in
the harbour and we are ashore with
only a 30minute delay to our schedule.

Unaware of compromises we board our bus.
The young guide tells us that young people
are moving here to this inhospitable place
where it is safer, there is less poverty and
tax breaks are offered to counteract the
affects of climate.

Today it is very warm at 23⁰C with only
a light breeze. This brings out the families
on this Sunday during the school holidays
and creates chaos.

The main routes out of town are dirt roads
It is too expensive to get materials down here
for any different surfacing. This place began
as a penal colony. The prisoners developed
the infrastructure one tree at a time.

Voyager

Later successful attempts were made to tame
the town and oil, gas, copper and tourism
all helped.

In the Tierra del Fuego National Park
we are closest to any remaining natural forest
with three types of Beech that are attacked
by insects and other parasites.

Balls of green, 'false mistletoe', adorn these
trees like Christmas decorations and beardy
lichen thrives.

There are no lizards or frogs here this is not
now the climate for them.

The bus drives down to the Beagle Channel
or Onashaga, part of the border between Chile
and Argentina.

Here we find 'The End of the World Post Office'
It is not true but it attracts visitors like moths
and the small car park cannot cope with today's
explosion of vehicles.

Once released from the confines of the bus, we
join a swarm of others, pushing and shoving
each other like each one is the only one with
the right of way.

How can this be leisure?

John S. Langley

A lady in a small bikini sunbathes in the midst as
if she were alone. Her tan is doing well except for
places best not to mention.

Amongst this confusion a Chimango Caracara hawk
golden, resplendent in the sun that lights it back
swoops and sweeps between rock and tree.

There are mussels aplenty clinging to the rocks in the
clear salt water.

Habitation here has been shown to go back at least
6,500 years, nomadic peoples feeding sustainably
on fish, seals and sea lions, using the animal skins
for coverings, the teeth and bones
for tools and adornment.

Later Indigenous people lived naked by choice even
in such a hostile climate, their skin daubed in natural
pastes, before they were 'civilised'.

The last of a pure blood tribal line died of Covid. She
was about 90 years old. So recently has one more
human chapter ended.

The car park gridlock is solved by perseverance and
20 minutes of unavoidably lost time by bus drivers
driving a convoluted tango of moves and probably
wishing they were somewhere else with someone else
on a day like today.

Voyager

Cars are parked all the way up one side of the track
so that the two way road becomes one way for two way
traffic!

We exit in a cloud of dust and travel on in a convoy
of buses generating its own ochre coloured storm
that permeates the ventilation system and dries out
our eyes and chokes our throat.

In this way we race on with flying commentary towards
the end of the Pan-America highway, past an obliviously
oozing peat bog, cone-topped mountains smeared with
snow, a U-shaped glacial valley and the wide Lapataia*
river and lakes that contain three varieties of Trout.

Through the dust we see cars strewn about the roadside
like an untidy disused car lot and camping sites, walking
routes, that on other days must be nice when, the day is
not so overcrowded.

When we reach Lapataia* Bay, or 'the bay of good wood'
'wild' horses (wouldn't you be?) are huddled under trees.

They are being photographed from every angle and must
be wondering why, all of a sudden, they are so popular.

John S. Langley

Now released from our tour
we thank the guide
and are shepherded
'This way, please.
Keep left.
Boarded walk is only 300 yards.
Watch your step.
Thank you for your visit.
We hope you enjoyed the tour
and that the rest of your time
will be good. Keep left
yes sir
that is left.
Have a nice day.'

Lapataia is pronounced Lap-it-tie-ya

Voyager

John S. Langley

Getting up Close

We board the Catamaran
120 keen passengers.

We see a sea otter rollicking
not far from the dock

The Captain races as we go
on deck, sea legs in place.

At the first stop sea lions ignore
the clicking of our cameras.

The male is large compared to
the females and youngsters.

He lolls, temporarily confident
in his position of authority.

There are other things too.

Cormorants pretend to be penguins
but aren't cormorants either.

They are Shags of the Imperial
and Rock variety.

But decorum dictates and who
are we to make a correction.

Voyager

A Chilean Skua sweeps the colony
looking for an easy meal.

A pair of Kelp geese, male dazzlingly
white, female demure and complex.

A Black Vulture, somehow menacing
shows itself, then moves on.

And finally, unexpectedly, on the same
small rocky islet as the lighthouse

a single Magellanic Penguin! Chest
double-barred.

The boat circles until we have all seen.
Although disturbed I hope we did
no lasting damage.

Back inside one fellow passenger
tells us he has the Premium Plus
Drinks Package.

He has made some new friends
from Austria and gets them all
their drinks.

John S. Langley

It's got to be nice to have made
new friends so easily.

A rainbow precedes a little rain
as we huddle together ready
to get off

a few spots wet us, like tears
as we wait for the tender...

Voyager

AROUND THE HORN (CHILE)

9th Jan 2023
18ºC   Sunrise: 04:48hrs   Sunset: 21:09hrs

Cape Horn

Here, at the end of the world
the furthest South we will ever go
we awake to a placid sea and
the onboard internet is working.

Albatrosses point our way.
We have no need to hold on to
the Ship's rail for balance
we ride the swell easily

Cape Horn is an island within a
group of islands. Here a Chilean
family is part way through an 18
month stint. I hope they stay friends.

We see the monument to the Albatross
the shape cut through plates of steel
air where the bird should be, a phantom
that must whistle in winds that do not

blow today. So many stories of this place
so many disasters, shipwrecks, anxiety
but today we look from our stable balcony
knowing a hot breakfast awaits.

John S. Langley

Voyager

We are shadowed by another cruise ship.
Even here, at the end of the world, tourism
is big business. Have we turned Cape Horn
into just another tourist attraction?

Surely on other days Nature must hold sway
and Cruise Ships keep their distance as the
sea and wind roll and rock and break in
white plumes of ice cold water

We have been lucky to pass on such a tame
day, are amazed we are actually here, a child-
hood ambition fulfilled, a moment to savour
before passing on into an open sea.

Later some Scottish passengers are talking
about money, about how much things cost
about how much they have spent, about how
much they have saved, whilst partaking of a
full breakfast and a bottomless coffee pot.

John S. Langley

Rolling Along

Once more
out of sight
of land
the Ship
rolls along
and we
roll with it.

SKI-ing

'We're SKI-ing,' she said
We looked blank
'Spending the Kids Inheritance,'
she said with a smile.
'They don't need it, if we spend it
they don't get it.'
Thinking about it I guess
we are doing the same thing.
But was that the right way
to think about it?

Would our kids
begrudge us this cruise?
I can't say we 'deserve' it
We just did
what we had to do
did what we could
the best way we could.

It's a sad sign of the times
in our part of the world
that inheritance matters
when in so many other places
there is so little to pass on.

John S. Langley

It didn't matter as much
to our generation
Thank Goodness!
Now when the kids ask
how we're feeling
we don't know
which answer
they would most appreciate.

We try to put the question
out of our minds
The sun is shining
we're in the Atlantic Ocean
maybe the boat could sink... !?

THE FALKLAND ISLANDS (U.K)

10th Jan 2023
11ºC   Sunrise: 04:48hrs   Sunset: 21:08hrs

John S. Langley

Approach

The approach is calm
there are penguins
on a beach of white sands
Turkey Buzzards spiralling

An artillery piece is visible atop
a ridge as a stark reminder of
an 80's thing that the penguins
must have wondered about

Spanish announcements on the
Ship PA still call this place Las
Malvinas as I'm pretty sure they
always will.

Such a small territory to be so
hotly disputed. A political pawn?
A distraction from other matters?
A question of National pride?

A strategic military marine position?
Or the incumbent rights to a piece
of Antarctica and future resources?
People died... that's all I know for sure.

The anchor chain is now down, forged
strong though browned with salt rust
tight to the bottom holding us steady
holding us here for less than a day

Voyager

We see cars ashore and wonder how
they got there. We are warned that on
these islands bio-security is important
that we must not pollute this place
inadvertently and we check our bags.

We note the temperature: 10.5^oC
We note wind speed: 11.2 m/s (light)
We note weather conditions: Stable
Because we have time to wait.

Not all cruise ships get to disembark.
It is weather dependent.

We wait.

There is a medical emergency.

We wait as is only right.

Our tender is delayed, someone has
forgotten their pass card…

Finally we are underway to the sound
of someone coughing.

25 minutes later we set our feet on the
Falkland Islands jetty and walk
to firmer ground.

The total number of people on our Ship
is more than half the island's permanent
population.

War

It is Margaret Thatcher Day!
We drive out, past the bright painted houses
of white, yellow, blue, with red corrugated roofs.

The commentary is thorough.

The Islands have been UK territory since 1833
with a ping-pong history before that.

The International Airport is pointed out.

The importation of people on 2-3yrs contracts
is to fill temporary gaps in local skills.

People either love or hate living here and leave
foot-ware on stakes in the ground at Boot Hill if
they leave and sometimes return to retrieve it.

We move onto a gravel road and continue on
through moorland. On either side are bizarre
Stone Runs. These rough-edged, rough-stacked
boulders are 2m deep reminders of the hot and
cold cycling that occurred as the Earth's crust
formed millions of years ago.

It is difficult terrain. Although today it is dry and
sunny a strong wind blows cold. We zip up our
jackets and hold on to our hats. Our guide tells
us it's a nice day.

There are no sheep, the grazing too poor here
and there are no trees for cover.

1982 - Argentina was under a military dictatorship
1983 - would mark the 150th anniversary of UK
occupation of the Islands. Events were planned
to celebrate.

Talks between Argentina and Britain were being
mediated by the UN and the USA. The decision
if it were a decision, was that the Islands should
determine their own fate.

Margaret Thatcher, the UK's then Prime Minister
decreed that the will of the people should prevail
US President Ronald Reagan agreed and gave
his support to this.

The Falkland Islanders chose the UK.

The Argentine Navy was assembled.
A show of strength.
Nobody believed they would invade.

The military strength of the Islands was paltry.
A few professionals backed by a Dad's army.

The Argentinian Forces invaded.

Whether they expected to walk in unmolested
is unsure.

There was fighting and short lived resistance
in Port Stanley.

The first People died.

Such action could not be tolerated.

The Falklands war of April-June 1982 began.

The 1,850 population of the Islands were subject to Argentine occupying forces.

The UK Navy was deployed, including helicopters Ships and, crucially, Nuclear Submarines.

Ordnance and people were deployed and destroyed on both sides.

Relics still remain rusting by the roadside.

'Yomps' or moving at 'Your Own Marching Pace' were carried out at night because of the lack of natural cover.

There were a series of attack and defend engagements.

French made Exocet missiles did their work wreaking havoc, sinking ships, drowning and burning human beings.

The UK forces made progress, the Argentines moved backwards.

A UK Nuclear Submarine sunk the Belgrano.

The Argentinian navy had no answer to this threat and were forced to stand clear of the exclusion zone.

But this was real, there were casualties on
both sides, two posthumous VC's awarded.

On West Falkland they listened avidly to the
radio reports.

Our tour guide was one of these people.

And this was war - there were errors.

His voice is steady as he re-tells his story.
Bad intelligence reported Argentinian military
activity on his farm, that they were forming
a base, a staging post, a threat.
It was all incorrect.

So when he heard the sound of aeroplanes
he opened his door to two low flying
Sea Harriers 'looking unfriendly'
carrying missiles.

One is fired.

Luckily for him a sturdily built wooden shed is
in the line of fire.

It takes a lot of the blast and is obliterated.

But it does not stop everything.

Our guide is blown backwards
pieces of shrapnel enter his body.

Those that could not be removed remain to this day
in his right wrist and in his head

after passing through his left eye
and damaging it beyond repair.

'That's war,' he says, 'and we're blessed with
two eyes. You just get used to missing one.'

The error was soon recognised.
He was airlifted to military hospital.

'There was nothing friendly about this fire,'
he says.

Weeks later, after the war is over, the pilot
of the Sea Harrier pays a visit to his farm.
He comes to apologise.
He brings wine and a good bottle of whisky.

They are still friends to this day.
The Sea Harrier pilot returned to attend his
wedding.

By June 15th 1982 the war was over.
The Islands were liberated.

We return to Stanley.

Last year was the 40th Anniversary
(the year less than two weeks over).

The War Memorial is decked in poppy wreaths.

The Falkland Islands is still
a British Overseas Territory.

John S. Langley

A recent vote recorded
that 99.7% of the population
want to keep it that way.

The Economy is good
based on Fishing, Tourism and Farming.
The population is increasing
and is now up to 3,662.
Young people can travel
to the UK
for A level and University
education.
75% come back.

Veterans return.
They are lauded.
The majority believe that...

                    the Falklands War was worth it.

Voyager

John S. Langley

Kathryn

A dear friend of ours died here
We pass the school we think
she worked in, the church she
would have attended.

A long way from Manchester.
A fresh adventure in an eventful life.
A new place, new friendships.
I think she was happy here.

Kathryn leaves a lasting legacy
in her children and in my memory
of a conversation on a foggy beach
about life and wished for futures

Life rarely takes you where you plan
and what you've always wanted
does not always turn out to be
what you've always wanted ...

John S. Langley

Gifts

Stanley has been designated a city.
Possibly the smallest city in the world?

Electricity is supplied
from a small diesel power station

or now there are 6 small wind turbines
which, on a good day, supply a third of
Stanley's needs.

There is no shortage of wind.

There are geese on the football pitch.
The phone boxes are red.

Tourists are being increasingly catered for.
There are Gift Shops, Cafes
a small open-air museum.

We take photos, send a postcard, wondering
which of us will get home first.

We buy Falkland's wool, Tea towels
a jumper (the only size XL in Stanley)
a woollen headband

Finally we are shepherded into line
for the tender back to the Ship
or be left behind.

I wonder fleetingly
how bad an option
that would be.

Voyager

John S. Langley

Farewell

Leaving we see no sheep!

Again Penguins
probably King Penguin
line the shore
but too far away
to be sure.

We wave to nobody
just a gesture
a mixture of
regret
thankfulness
and farewell

Off-shore a Minke whale
rises to the surface
sleek grey-black skin
curved dorsal fin
it blows
and breathes
and dives

Before it surfaces again
we have moved on.

Later

We eat like gluttons
chicken curry with rice
pork filled tacos with salsa and sour cream
pancakes with chocolate sauce
and a glass full of Chilean white wine

It's the first time we've done this
taken such advantage.
I hope we can stop.

The evening entertainment
is from Buenos Aires
a Gaucho show
of Flamenco and Bolas
to the rhythm of Bomobos

The Falklands War is not mentioned
Instead the four Argentinian dancers
show, on a huge screen, a photograph
of Lionel Messi holding up the World Cup

Times change
and they will change again.

AT SEA

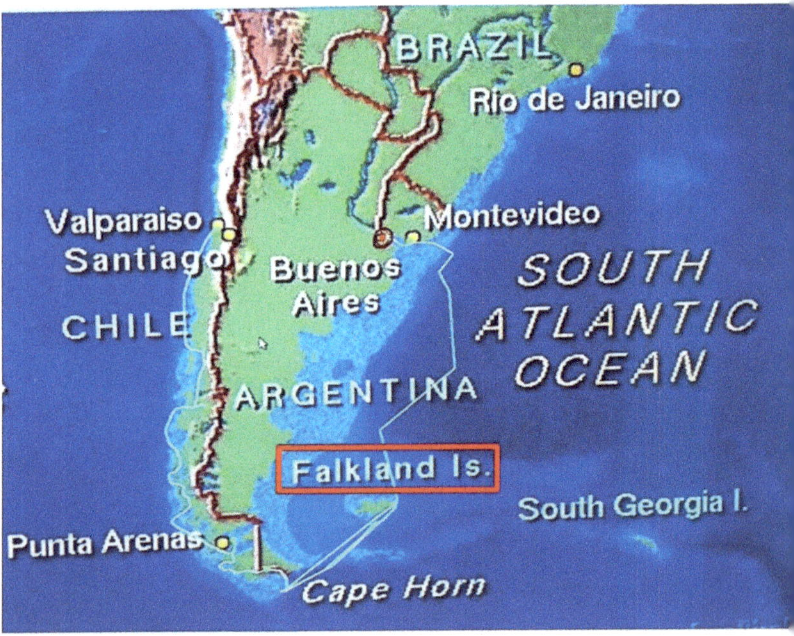
BRAZIL
Rio de Janeiro
Valparaiso
Santiago
Montevideo
Buenos Aires
SOUTH ATLANTIC OCEAN
CHILE
ARGENTINA
Falkland Is.
South Georgia I.
Punta Arenas
Cape Horn

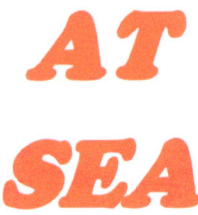

Voyager

John S. Langley

Course Correction

We wake to fog
the resonant sound
of the Ship's horn
booming out
intermittently

It is a white out

Later the Captain:
A weather system
a deep low
is in our path
at its heart
is heavy rain
hurricane force winds
of 100mph
and 10m waves

The choice is
to carry on or
to change course
to avoid it

The Captain has decided
he cannot risk the safety
of the Ship

so with regret
we will change course
go further out

Voyager

into the Atlantic
to stay 600 nautical miles
away from the storm

We will not make
our next port of
Puerto Madryn.
We will be at sea
for three days.

It is a stark reminder
that we are not in control
of everything

The power of Nature
far exceeds our own

We switch on the TV.
The onboard information channel
displays a caption
'Enjoy this beautiful day at sea'!

John S. Langley

Right Decision?

This Ship does this cruise twice only
every year.

Once from East to West
then from West to East

We are on the latter.
Neither cruise will have been
completed as planned.

At the first attempt the Ship
failed to visit
the Falkland Islands
and Punta Arenas.
We will fail to visit
Puerto Madryn.

I am happy to have been on this cruise!

But does this mean that
this is an impossible task?
That this cruise cannot be
completed because, over
such a distance and so many
days, the weather will always
intervene at least once?

Voyager

Or is our Italian Captain too
risk averse? Does he take
avoiding action too easily
rather than lesser course
corrections that would still
see us reach our ports of call?

Certainty when he made his
announcement he said that
some would disagree but that
he was the Captain and he
must make the decision.

Surely safety first, for Ship
crew and passengers is the
right priority.

But there is risk in everything
we do and the line between
acceptable and unacceptable
is blurred and grey.

Was this the right decision?
We will never know and besides
what does 'right' mean?

John S. Langley

Change of Direction

We are travelling North and getting warmer
The layers of clothing are reducing

Our side of the ship now faces West
so we can watch the Sun set.

We reflect that travelling towards home
has its advantages.

The Sunset begins before it begins
casting a yellow glow on the under
side of the broken cloud lines that
are turning grey. Blue can still be seen
above and through gaps
in the clouds.

The sea reflects the changing palate
undulating in yellow peaks and grey
blue troughs.

At 8:59pm the last small segment of
Sun disappears into the water horizon

Over the next 50minutes as we watch
the colours morph seamlessly through
yellow, to orange to crimson and on to
a spectrum of red-greys

At this point the planet Mercury sparks
star white in a gap in the cloud close to
the horizon, the only real gap in the clouds.

We watch it fall and 16 minutes after we
first see it, it sets into the billowing sea.

Voyager

It is now 1hr and 6mins after Sunset
and the sky darkens to fall into night

the higher cloud masks the heavens
the stars are hidden

we go back inside.

It has been a gloriously immersive experience.

John S. Langley

PUERTO MADRYN

- THE MISSED STOP

At Last

In the Breakfast restaurant
there are tables and
there are tables.

The ones by the windows
have padded bench seats
like a private booth

They are desirable, prized
and way beyond our lazy
morning start time

But today! Being later than
ever, we hit a moment when
one has come free!

Aah... the comfort! At last the
ability to revel in the jealous looks
of other passengers

that do not include us! The coffee
tastes better, the toast crisper and
we ask the waiter
                    ... to take his time.

John S. Langley

The Stop We Missed

We are travelling slowly.

We have plenty of time now
before we are due to dock
in Montevideo

The Ship is eating up time
as if there were too much
of it.

It is not unusual to plan to
go somewhere and not to
make it.

'C'est la vie' as I learnt in my
school French and later from
experience.

Although in Puerto Madryn you
could see more of Patagonia's
Flora and Fauna

and be surprised by the Welsh
immigrant legacy in place names
and local DNA

Voyager

we had opted to see the Dinosaur
discoveries that are apparently
incredible to behold

which we now won't see although
we now have time to contemplate
the impermanence

of what we consider set in stone.
A reminder, if we needed it, that
change is permanent.

The Dinosaurs have moved on from
their port of call, we have to watch
that we don't miss ours.

John S. Langley

Walking

We try and walk at least 5,000 steps a day
although I'm sure my step counter misses
a few.

On Sea Days this means us walking around
Deck 7 anticlockwise from starboard to bow
to port to stern in a stately manner

This is not always easy! The Ship can roll, the
wind can gust (we don't go out if it's raining)
and we totter rather than walk

We need to do this circuit three or four times
to get close. Some people go clockwise, others
walk a lot faster and pass us

though we have not yet been lapped. And a few
well, one or two, dawdle and we pass them
but that doesn't happen often.

Voyager

John S. Langley

Position on the Map

So I was wrong
5hrs difference to New York
8hrs to Los Angeles
but only 3 to Santiago
on the West Coast
of South America

And I thought
they were equally far away

Voyager

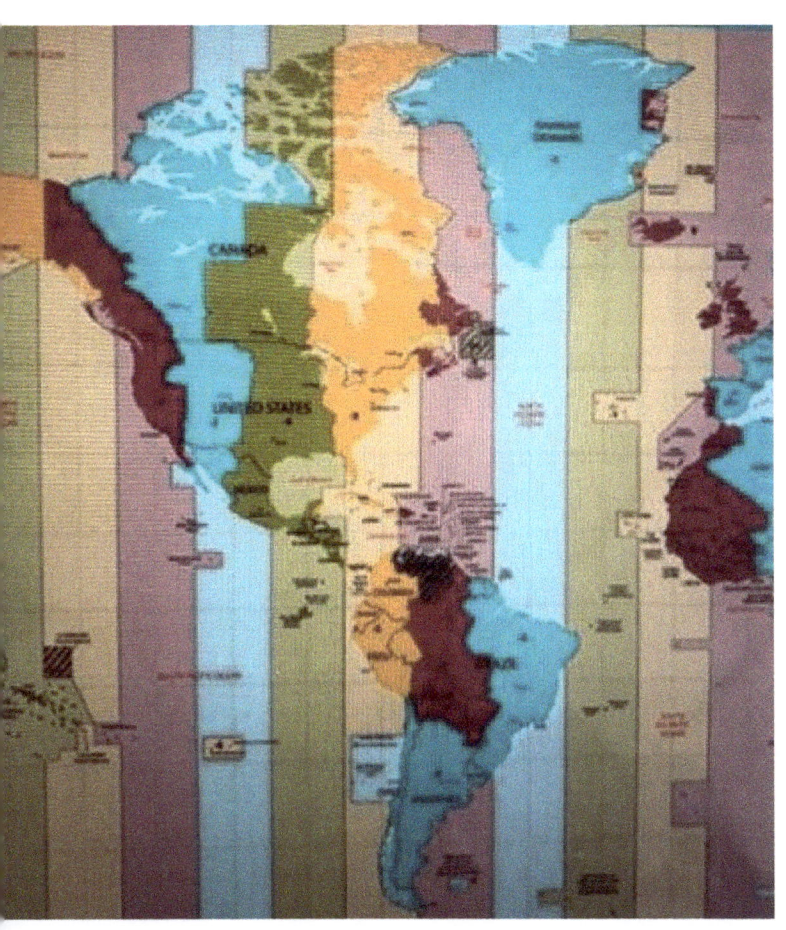

John S. Langley

Something They Agree On

The countries we are visiting have a history
of not agreeing on very much.

But, I was surprised to find, they all agree on
something quite fundamental

They agree on the clock. There is no time
difference between Chile,

Argentina, the Falkland Islands and Uruguay
despite their differences

in language and culture they all agree to abide
by the same artificial division of time

It all starts with the man-made division of a circle
into $360°$ (why 360? why not 100?)

It's only a number, that is exactly divisible by 24
the chosen number of hours in a day

but why not 36? Why not 18? And in our minutes
and number of seconds

why the love of 60? Why not 100? It is shown to be daft because

we record the fastest 100m time in seconds and decimal points!

The first number is part of a system of 60 and the others that follow the decimal point are

in a system of 10's. And yet here are 4 countries that agree they can accept

these strange divisions. If they accept that then why not a lot more...

John S. Langley

The Lift Expert

'That one's going down' he said.
I could see that.
'And we want to go up.'
This much was true.
'I always have to wait when
I want to go up,' he said
This was not always our experience
but I nodded all the same.
'I am sure,' he said, 'that more
of these lifts go down than up.'
I thought about this
pictured a pile of concertinaed
lift compartments at
the bottom of the lift shafts
a busy gang of engineers
at the top madly constructing
new compartments
to drop in, hoping that no one
would notice the discrepancy.

A lift pinged its arrival.
It was going up.
The man stepped towards
the smoothly opening doors
'After you,' I said, 'You take
this one, we'll take the next.'
The doors shushed closed
on his astonished face
'Nice talking to you,' I muttered
'safe trip.'

Voyager

Dinner Conversation

We met an 87 year old Argentinian man
who was on the cruise with his 75 year old
little sister.

His English was much better than my
Spanish - to my shame.

He had had a scholarship to the States.
He asked where we were from, there was
a misunderstanding, he thought we were
American. I did not correct him.

He told me about his time in the States
as if I would recognise the landmarks.
I smiled and nodded. I think his sister
realised the mistake but didn't or couldn't
correct him.

We talked of the cruise, a mutual highlight
was the Islands, Malvinas to him Falklands
to me.

Voyager

They had visited the Argentinian cemetery.
I told him we had been on the Battlefield Tour.
We agreed it was poignant, we agreed that
people died, that both sides had lives to mourn.

When we parted we shook hands, smiled at
each other and waved as the distance between
us increased.

.....

*When we were waiting in Buenos Aires airport
I went for a walk around, we had plenty of time.
Memorials to the war and the difficulty in
establishing an Argentinian Cemetery on the
Islands afterwards were hidden away on an
upper level where few people went.*

John S. Langley

Parasitic Jaeger

We are sailing over 4,000 feet of water
A bird sweeps through the boundary layer
between water and sky

We watch and notice behaviour, markings
it is a magnificent aerial acrobat
we look it up in a book

It has been named 'Parasitic Jaeger' it skims
oblivious over a smooth sea more beautifully
marked than its name suggests

Who named this bird? I apologise on behalf
of the human race. It deserves a much better
name even if it knows nothing of this

In the North where they still breed we are kinder
and name them Arctic Skua. It is only on migrating
South to chase warmth that their name changes

We choose to ignore one of theirr clever means
of feeding, the chasing of other birds until they
regurgitate and then feasting on the vomit

Clever bird, well adapted, skilled aerobat
distinctively marked, you do not know nor care
about your name which, if any other, would
smell as sweet

Voyager

A mixed school of dolphins break the surface
Long Finned Pilot Whales amongst them ride
the swell, jumping, communing, oblivious of my
internal debate, my feelings of complicity.

John S. Langley

Sorry

Sorry, we're British
So we are used to apologising
It is a national characteristic.

If two of us bump into each other
we will both apologise
'I'm sorry.'
'No I'm sorry.'
'No, really, I'm sure it was me.'
'I really must insist...'

So please don't apologise to me
over some trivial thing unless
you're a member of the club
after all our history it's just about
all we have left, that and our
sense of humour.

I hope I haven't offended you
by this explanation
maybe I shouldn't have
written this down...
     ... sorry...

MONTEVIDEO

(Uruguay)

14th Jan 2023
30ºC   Sunrise: 05:58hrs   Sunset: 19:57hrs

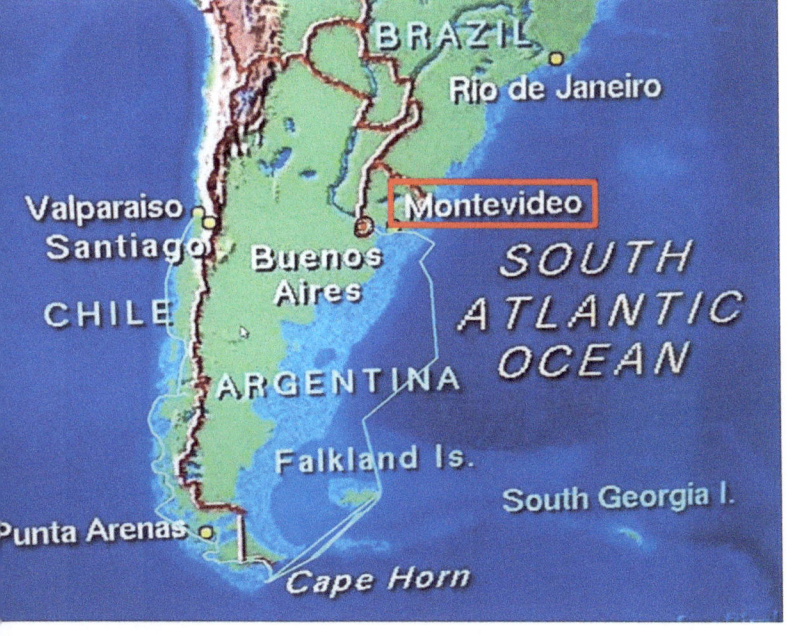

John S. Langley

Not What We Expected

We have docked
No tenders this time
Montevideo is hot
the buses are queued

When we visited Buenos Aires
they told us Montevideo was like
a poor cousin, that they were less
sophisticated, poorer and not
as clean.

We had nothing else to believe
so we took it all in.

It is not true.

Montevideo is a clean city, there
are a few beggars but no more
than anywhere else, and they are
not aggressive.

The city conjures up memories
of European architecture and
 influences.

The people are friendly and
understanding of our lack of
Spanish.

Voyager

Prices approximately double
for tourists but, hey, that's what
we're here for, to spend money
and contribute to their economy.

Right now they've pretty much
got their act together. Trapped
between two big brothers Brazil
and Argentina they know it's best
to stay friends.

John S. Langley

Sizes

Argentina's population is over 45 million
with over 13 million in Buenos Aires
about 30%

Brazil's population is 214 million

Uruguay has a population of 3.5 million
with nearly 1.8 million in Montevideo
about 50%

The population of London is around 9 million
about 14% of the UK total

and over 2.5 times the total population
 of Uruguay

We Scratch the Surface

We are here during the long school summer holidays
December 20th to 1st March so the city empties onto
the beaches. We drive past, there is fishing off the sands
many lines. We see a catch taken.

A modern city that has been Portuguese, Spanish,
even British in its history and became independent in 1825
Since 1985 after a military dictatorship, Democracy has
returned. A President, two political parties, they swing
between them.

There are many apartment blocks with expensive
apartments at $3,000 a square metre and a myriad of air
conditioning units, an Opera theatre - Teatro Solis
Protesters in Independence Square on hunger strike
their flags representing different groups of workers.

The streets are lined with Sycamore Trees giving shade
McDonalds has successfully invaded – the teenagers like it
There is graffiti, some of it art, some to protest

We drive past the ranks of shops, restaurants, banks

Carnival is coming they are getting ready
It lasts for 40 nights
There were African domestic slaves.
% of the population is of Afro descent
Now their music is played as part of the Carnival

John S. Langley

There is a 'free' tax funded health care system
The Economy is based on farming; including
Sugar cane oranges, barley, cheese, and rice
and notably 12 millions cows

The minimum salary is $472, 8.3% are unemployed
VAT is 22% and inflation is at 8.3%

28% of exports, mainly meat and cellulose paper
go to China,16% to Brazil, 5% to the USA

We pass an open street market selling fresh food
fruit, vegetables, fish.

and down by the sea a panoramic view of the city
and parakeets in eucalyptus trees

We drive back along the coastal road, La Rambla
and are told about Uruguayan food and wine

Montevideo is more modern, more upbeat
cleaner and with a better standard of living
than we expected.

We have time to walk around before getting
back on the ship, to witness the giant flame grill
barbecues, with meat of all kinds, done to your
particular taste.

Voyager

It is 32 ºC, the bus was comfortable
with great legroom and air conditioning

We have seen Parakeets, Oriole
Sparrow, Thrush, a swallow or martin
coursing over water

We buy T-shirts, leather gloves and
are asked for our feedback twice before we leave.
Did we enjoy our visit?

We did, it was eye-opener.

John S. Langley

The Last Ones

The indigenous peoples were dispossessed
the Indios Charruas finally massacred
by order because they were deemed to be
encroaching on farmer's and landowner's land.
Land that had been theirs.

The last few were rounded up and sent to Paris
where they were sold to a circus to be used
as exhibits.

Two escaped, a woman and a baby, no one
knows what happened to them.

They now have a bronze statue at the roadside
there is a tree with bright red flowers nearby.
It is a terrible story, told plainly.
Why have the statue?
Is it guilt? Does it make any difference?

Voyager

John S. Langley

Covid

On 13th march 2020 schools were closed
lockdowns began. It was tough.

Now restrictions are lifted thanks to
vaccinations.

With 3.5 million people the population was
vaccinated quickly.

The government message was very clear
– if you don't accept vaccinations then you die.

Now to have had 5 vaccinations is normal.

Masks were worn until mid 2022 and still are
in hospitals.

Cruise Ships disappeared.
There was only 1 cruise in 2022
and the people onboard were infected !

And so it is now and it is us!
Their tours have just restarted
We are in the vanguard!

Voyager

Our bus was full of coughing
we'd noticed it getting slowly worse
throughout the course of the cruise
and now there was

Coughing to the front of us
Coughing to the back of us
Coughing all around us

and in the face of this volley of germs
we put our face masks back on
and crossed our fingers.

BUENOS AIRES
(Argentina)

15th Jan 2023
36ºC   Sunrise: 06:07hrs   Sunset: 20:05hrs

John S. Langley

Disembarkation

It's as easy as this...

You put out your big bags
properly labelled
colour coded
no later than 11pm
the night before

You wake up at 6am
probably best to set
an alarm
go to breakfast
and then wait in your room

Remember to switch on
station 21 on your TV
and wait for announcements
When your colour code
is called you proceed

Probably to Deck 4
Probably at about 7:15
and you must make sure
you've settled your account
Did I not mention that?

Voyager

So sorry, and that's best done
the day before although the
Credit Desk is only open
certain hours, I can't recall
which ones

You can find that out
for yourselves although
you will not be allowed
off the Ship if this is not
sorted out properly

Now, what was I saying?
Oh, yes, at probably Deck 4
you will leave the Ship
checking out with your key card
for the last time

Remember to have all your
valuables, paperwork and medication
with you in your hand baggage
which you will bring with you
Is that clear so far?

You will then hop on a transit bus
to take you to the Main Terminal
building. You may have to pick up
your big bags before the transit bus
but probably not

John S. Langley

When you reach the Main Terminal
building you will probably then
re-unite yourself with your big bags
either way you will need to have these
as you proceed to Immigration

Have your passport ready
and once through this then
look out for signs for buses
with your colour code to
take you to the Airport

If you don't find any
don't panic
just try and find someone
who might be willing
to help

It's really just as easy as that...
We hope you've enjoyed your cruise
see you again soon
and, oh, I almost forgot
Any questions?

There's only one thing

There's only one thing
we need the Ship's internet for
and that's to do online check-in
for the flight home

It has worked more or less fine
the whole cruise. Only now
when we really need it, it has
gone awol!

All of a sudden there is no-one
to help. Somewhere, in the same
ether as the internet somebody
is trying to fix it

We cannot be told who it is, we
cannot be told how long it will
take to resolve, we just have to
wait, hope and trust

With so much time in hand I
decided to write this poem.
It hasn't helped...

John S. Langley

GOING HOME

Knowing When To...

A 12 and a half hour flight
overnight with little sleep
A 3hr time difference
the wrong way for an
early morning landing

I tried to correct, to edit
some of the poems for
this collection but my
head was in a fog, the
only thing I could do was

make things worse, lose
the plot, forget what I'd
been trying to say, between
the lines, so I just had to ...

John S. Langley

Taking for Granted

My headset was not working properly

Taking for granted that I was 40,000 feet up
in the air where no human being
is designed to be

Taking for granted that I was warm, dry and
cocooned at a height I should be freezing cold
going at double the speed of the fastest Ferrari

Taking for granted that the seat was comfortable
the leg room sufficient, I had just been given a
hot towel to sooth myself, alcohol and pretzels

Taking for granted that I was going to be in a
different hemisphere, across the mighty Atlantic
Ocean in less than twelve hours time

Taking for granted all that and that I had an
entertainment system at my seat and a three
course meal to come, despite all that, I was
upset that my headset wasn't working properly
that the sound was distorted... I mean, come on...

I mentioned it to the Stewardess.
She found a replacement.
It worked perfectly.
All was sweetness and light.

Voyager

John S. Langley

Back

We are leaving Buenos Aires
when the outside temperature
is 36 ºC

We travel at an average height of 41,000 ft
With an outside temperature of -54 ºC
Our ground speed is 580mph

When we get home it is -4 ºC
there is a little lying snow
two Roe Deer appear fleetingly
in the road in front of us
their white bums flashing

I'm pleased I bought such
a lot of woolen clothing
to bring home with us.

Even though most of it
is decorated with penguins.

Voyager

REFLECTIONS

John S. Langley

Leisure Domes

We build ourselves pleasure domes
hotels, stadia, cruise ships...

Each new arrival trying to be the best
outdo the last, cost more, be more
lavish.

And we get to timeshare in these
places, paying enough to profit
the owners

If there are any imperfections we
complain, though our own homes
are much worse

It is a remarkable part of our culture
that vast numbers work to provide
these comforts to others

that they will never meet, never know
but whose money will pay for their
own holidays in turn

In a different leisure dome.

Is it not so?

In the so-called 'Developed World'

We are
no longer hunter-gatherers

We are
no longer subsistence farmers

We exist
in uncomfortably large societal groups

We have
distanced ourselves from our own eco-system

Nothing
gets away with that for long

Under stress
we will revert, uncomfortably at first

If we
do not act collectively and voluntarily

Then Natural Forces will do it for us.

John S. Langley

What have we learnt?

I.

That we are privileged
to be able to afford
once in our lives
to come on a cruise
like this

II.

That if you pay enough money
you are elevated in the society
that exists onboard, irrespective
of background, colour, creed or
whether this was easy money or
you've spent every last dime of
your life savings.

For this you get more space, a
beautiful view, you need never
leave your suite as you have your
own concierge who brings all
you ask for to your table, books
your tickets for you, escorts you
to the front of the queue or the
best seats, is a kind of bodyguard
clearing the way through us plebs
and cleans up after you.

Is this Democracy in action?
Is this the Market Economy
at its most fruitful?
Is this giving the right impression?
That if you have enough money
then any problem can be solved
for you... is this why our solution to
climate change is Carbon Credits?
That our Western way out of the
drowning of Pacific Islands is to
pay compensation?
Is the World a bank in which we
can manage the Profit and Loss
with dollar bills?

III.

That this world is beautiful
and endlessly fascinating
though red in tooth and claw
That it is not tamed
That we are not it's masters

IV.

That we privileged few
can feast upon the waves
everything provided
within easy reach

John S. Langley

as much as you want
when you want
in a controlled environment
a heated/cooled cabin

V.

That even the biggest Ship
rolls on the sea

VI.

or nothing?

www.ingramcontent.com/pod-product-compliance
Lightning Source LLC
Chambersburg PA
CBHW041141110526
44590CB00027B/4091